CIVIL WAR
HIGHLIGHTS

CAUSES
OF THE WAR
1800–1861

TIM COOKE

The UNITED STATES

4c

POSTAGE

Those who Deny
freedom to others
Deserve it not
for Themselves.

A. Lincoln

OF AMERICA

Credo

A⁺
Smart Apple Media

This edition published in 2013 by
Smart Apple Media, an imprint of Black Rabbit Books
PO Box 3263, Mankato, MN 56002

www.blackrabbitbooks.com

Brown Bear Books Ltd.
Editorial Director: Lindsey Lowe
Managing Editor: Tim Cooke
Children's Publisher: Anne O'Daly
Picture Manager: Sophie Mortimer
Creative Director: Jeni Child

Library of Congress Cataloging-in-Publication Data
Causes of the war : 1860-1861 / edited by Tim Cooke.
      p. cm. -- (Civil War highlights)
 Includes bibliographical references and index.
 Summary: "In an almanac-like format, outlines the causes of the US Civil
War, including the issues of slavery and states' rights. Also discusses the
political environment and events that spurred the war, such as the elec-
tion of Abraham Lincoln and the Raid on Harpers Ferry"--Provided by
publisher.
 ISBN 978-1-59920-813-8 (library binding)
1. United States--History--Civil War, 1861-1865--Causes--Juvenile literature. 2. Slavery--Southern States--History--Juvenile literature. I. Cooke,
Tim, 1961-
 E459.C365 2013
 973.7'11--dc23
                                2012001162

Printed in the United States of America at Corporate Graphics,
North Mankato, Minnesota

PO1437
2-2012

9 8 7 6 5 4 3 2 1

Picture Credits

Front Cover: TopFoto: The Granger Collection

Corbis: 14, 28; Bettmann 26, 31; **Library of Congress:** 5, 7, 10,
12, 13, 15, 18, 19, 20, 21, 23, 25, 27, 29, 30, 32, 33, 34, 35,
39, 40, 41, 42; **National Archives of America:** 6, 11, 16, 37;
Robert Hunt Library: 8, 24, 36; **Thinkstock:** Comstock 38;
Photos.com 4, 17, 22

All Artworks: Windmill Books.

Contents

Introduction

The war that broke out in 1861 divided the whole United States. Its roots lay in a practice that had been going on in North America for nearly 250 years: slavery.

Slavery was not the only cause of the war—but it was the most important one. Millions of black slaves had been shipped to North America and sold to work, usually on large farms called plantations. Most plantations were in the South. The North had smaller farms, and more industry. Many Northerners believed that owning slaves was wrong.

The North and the South were divided by more than just slavery. The North had far more people, many of whom lived in cities. In the South, many people did not want the North to interfere in their lives via the laws of the federal government.

From the mid–19th century, divisions between the North and South grew wider. As settlers headed west, territories

This picture of slave children near their homes shows an idealized version of slave life.

A white planter oversees black workers on a cotton plantation in Mississippi.

applied to join the Union. Northerners thought any new states should be free states; in the South, people thought that new states should allow slavery.

A series of compromises temporarily put off a split over slavery. But then Northern Abolitionists began to campaign for slavery to be banned everywhere. The lines were drawn. When the antislavery Republican Abraham Lincoln was elected as president in 1860, war became inevitable.

This book

Causes of the War describes how tensions grew from 1800 until war began in 1861. It examines the nature of slavery in the South, and the campaign to have it abolished. A timeline across the bottom of the pages throughout the book traces important developments from 1800 to 1865, including not just events related to slavery but also events beyond the United States. At the back of the book is a Need to Know feature, which will help you relate subjects to your studies at school.

What Caused the War?

As 1861 began, many Americans realized that the country would soon be at war. But the two sides—the North and the South—did not agree on what had brought them to such a position.

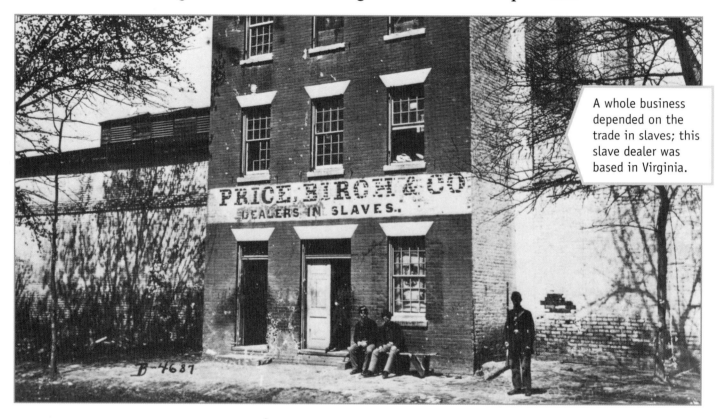

A whole business depended on the trade in slaves; this slave dealer was based in Virginia.

At the end of 1860, a number of states in the South had decided to secede, or leave the Union. For people in the North who believed that the Union should be kept together, secession was an act of treason. It was the task of President

1800–1805

UNITED STATES

1800 VIRGINIA Inspired by the Baptist Church, Gabriel Prosser plans a slave uprising; it is crushed before it takes place.

1801 WASHINGTON, D.C. Thomas Jefferson becomes the third president of the United States; he calls slavery a "necessary evil," but predicts that it will eventually die out.

OTHER EVENTS

1801 GREAT BRITAIN The Act of Union creates the United Kingdom of Great Britain and Ireland.

1801 HAITI Former slave Toussaint Louverture declares himself ruler of independent Haiti.

1800   1801   1802

Abraham Lincoln to defend the Union, by warfare if
necessary. They did not think that states could choose to
leave the United States. In the South, the view was very
different. Secessionists were angry that Lincoln had
been elected president in 1860. He was against slavery,
which was common in the South. To Southerners, the
fact that the president opposed their way of life meant
that the "United" States did not actually feel very
united. Many Southerners believed that they had to
quit the Union in order to defend what they saw as
their right to choose how they should live.

A divisive issue

Whatever both sides claimed, the main issue that
divided them was slavery. The *Charleston Mercury* had
written in 1858, "On the subject of slavery the North
and South are not only two Peoples, but they are rival,
hostile Peoples." There were about 3.5 million black
slaves in the South. Most of them worked on plantations to
grow crops such as tobacco, rice, and cotton. Cotton was in
great demand on the world market, and cotton plantations
dominated the Southern economy. In the North, meanwhile,
slavery had been abolished in 1804.

This poster
supports the Free
Soil Party, an anti-
slavery party led
by Martin van
Buren (left).

A growing country

The issue of slavery became more important during the first
half of the 19th century. The United States was expanding
rapidly. First, President Thomas Jefferson bought the
Lousiana Territory from France in 1803. That doubled the

1803 THE WEST The Louisiana
Purchase: the United States buys land
west of the Mississippi from France,
doubling the size of the country and
opening new territory to settlement.

1804 THE NORTH Slavery is abolished
in all states north of Maryland.

1805 EUROPE The French emperor
Napoleon Bonaparte defeats the
Austrians and Russians at the decisive
Battle of Austerlitz.

1803   1804   1805

Abraham Lincoln's inauguration as president in 1861 marked the coming of the crisis.

nation's size. Victory in the Mexican War (1846–1848) added another area of territory in the west and southwest. In both cases, settlers quickly moved into the new territories. As their frontier communities became organized and more people went to live there, they asked to become states of the Union. But would slavery be permitted in these new states?

The debate threatened to split the country, but in 1820 the so-called Missouri Compromise seemed to successfully put it off. It decreed that Missouri would enter the Union as a slave state; but at the same time, Maine in the North would be admitted as a free state. That would preserve the balance between free and slave states. In the remainder of the Louisiana Purchase, however, slavery was permanently excluded north of latitude 36° 30'.

QUAKER CAMPAIGN

The earliest opposition to slavery in America was led by Quakers. The Quakers followed a form of Christianity that argued that no one should have power over another human being. Such beliefs made them unpopular in Europe, so many moved to North America to practice their faith. There they led opposition to slavery.

The debate heats up

In the North, more people were beginning to believe that slavery was immoral. They thought that it had no place in a modern, Christian country. Some people began to campaign for the abolition of slavery. Those who supported this campaign were called abolitionists.

1806–1810

UNITED STATES

1806 WASHINGTON, D.C.
Congress authorizes the building of the first federal highway, the Great National Pike or Cumberland Road.

1807 WASHINGTON, D.C.
Congress passes an act prohibiting the importation of slaves into the United States, which comes into force from January 1, 1807.

1807 VIRGINIA Future Confederate commander Robert E. Lee is born at Stratford Hall, Virginia.

OTHER EVENTS

1806 CENTRAL EUROPE
The Holy Roman Empire comes to an end after 1,000 years.

1807 RUSSIA
Serfdom is abolished in Russia.

1807 GREAT BRITAIN
The slave trade is abolished in the British empire.

1806   1807

In the 1850s the debate grew more extreme. The more Northerners condemned slavery, the more Southerners stood up for what they called the "peculiar institution." Some even claimed that slavery was the natural condition of the "inferior" black race. Slavery was a blessing for slave as well as master.

War becomes inevitable

Three events in the decade made war inevitable. The first was the 1854 Kansas–Nebraska Act. Congress decided to allow the settlers in both states created by the act to decide whether slavery would be allowed. Kansas became a battlefield between supporters of slavery and Free Soilers (antislavery settlers).

Then, in 1857, the U.S. Supreme Court turned down a claim from Missouri slave Dred Scott to be set free. The court angered Northerners by ruling that the government had no power to ban slavery.

In November 1860, Lincoln was elected as president. For Southerners, his election confirmed their second-class status in the Union. Secession seemed the only answer. So the fateful step was taken. Now civil war was just around the corner.

This map shows which side each state took in the Civil War.

SLAVERY IN THE CONSTITUTION

There was little discussion of the future of slavery when the Founders drew up the U.S. Constitution in 1787. Although the institution of slavery ran against the founding principles of liberty and equality on which the new republic was based, slavery was not outlawed. "The thing is hid away in the Constitution," Abraham Lincoln said in 1854. Antislavery campaigners had to accept that the Constitution would not back their cause. Instead, they appealed to morality. In the words of New York senator William H. Seward, "There is a higher law than the Constitution."

1808 KENTUCKY Future Confederate president Jefferson Davis is born in Christian County, Kentucky.

1809 MASSACHUSETTS The Gothic writer Edgar Allan Poe is born in Boston, Massachusetts.

1808 SIERRA LEONE Britain takes responsibility for Sierra Leone in Africa, which opponents of slavery have chosen as a colony to resettle freed slaves from North America and Jamaica.

1808 SPAIN The British begin the Peninsular War against Napoleon Bonaparte in Spain.

1810 MEXICO The Catholic priest Miguel Hidalgo leads an unsuccessful uprising in Mexico against Spanish rule.

A "Peculiar Institution"

Southerners called slavery the "peculiar institution." They believed that people in the North who opposed slavery did not understand the unique role that it played in the South.

A slave is sold in Richmond, Virginia. Such sales often separated members of a slave family.

Many people in the South saw slavery in economic terms. By the middle of the 19th century, the Southern economy relied on the cheap labor of slaves. Abolition threatened to destroy the whole economy. In the North, people who were

1811–1815

UNITED STATES

1812 WASHINGTON, D.C.
The United States declares war on Britain (the War of 1812), provoked by continuing blockade of its ports and attacks on its shipping; U.S. forces invade Canada.

OTHER EVENTS

1811 VENEZUELA
Simón Bolivar declares Venezuela independent from Spain.

1811 GREAT BRITAIN
George, son of King George III of Britain, becomes prince regent when the king is declared insane.

1812 RUSSIA Napoleon invades Russia but bitter winter weather forces him to retreat from Moscow.

1811   1812   1813

against slavery stressed the moral debate. In 1858, Abraham Lincoln summed up the quarrel as being "between men who think slavery is wrong and those who do not."

Slaves were kept in this slave pen in Alexandria, Virginia, before they were sold at auction.

The slave trade

Slavery arrived in Spanish and Portuguese colonies in the New World before the 17th century. In North America, colonists forced Native Americans into slavery in both Virginia and New England. Native Americans were not considered to be good slaves, however. They got sick easily. As early as 1619, the first West African slaves landed at Jamestown, Virginia.

In the late 1700s, Americans won freedom from Britain in the Revolutionary War. Not everyone was free, however. The U.S. Constitution upheld the right of one human being to own another. Many of the Founders owned slaves themselves.

Already, Southern states used more slave labor than others. In South Carolina, slaves outnumbered the white population, for example. This reflected the dependence of the Southern states on large-scale plantation agriculture.

The abolition campaign

A movement to abolish slavery began in Britain in the 1780s. By 1800 many Americans were also becoming concerned about whether slavery was morally acceptable. In 1807 Britain

SONGS OF SLAVERY

One Southern argument was that slaves must be happy because they sang as they worked. When the abolitionist Frederick Douglass published his autobiography in 1845, he told a different story. According to Douglass, slaves did not sing because they were happy: "Slaves sing most when they are most unhappy. The songs of the slave represent the sorrows of his heart; and he is relieved by them, only as an aching heart is relieved by its tears."

1814 WASHINGTON, D.C.
British forces burn the White House during the War of 1812.

1814 ALABAMA/FLORIDA
U.S. forces defeat the Creek people, beginning the exclusion of Native Americans from the South.

1814 FRANCE Napoleon abdicates; the French monarchy is restored.

1815 INDONESIA Mount Tambora erupts in Indonesia. It kills more than 92,000 people and the ash it throws into the atmosphere causes the "year without a summer."

FREDERICK DOUGLASS

Born into slavery in 1818, and soon separated from his mother, Frederick Douglass escaped from slavery. He became a leader of the abolitionist movement. Douglass learned to read and write and used the written word to describe his life as a slave and argue his case against slavery.

abolished the slave trade throughout its empire. In the same year, the U.S. government banned its own Atlantic slave trade. By then slavery had been banned or was being phased out in all the U.S. states north of Delaware.

The changes made slavery an explosive issue. The United States was now clearly divided between slave states and free states. As Northerners campaigned to abolish slavery, Southerners defended their "peculiar institution."

Southern view of slavery

Many Southerners looked down on Northerners. They called them "Yankees," and caricatured them as greedy people only concerned with money. In contrast, they saw Southern life as far more civilized—thanks to slavery. They presented a picture of happy slaves singing in the cotton fields. That seemed more desirable than the lives of the "wage slaves" who worked day and night in the factories of the North.

Not everyone in the South owned slaves. In fact, only one in four whites were slave holders. Many whites had no slaves. Even farmers who did often worked alongside their slaves in the fields. It was also common practice for masters to hire out slaves who had particular practical skills.

This antislavery image shows a female slave being beaten as a punishment.

1816–1819

UNITED STATES

OTHER EVENTS

1816 WEST INDIES A slave revolt is put down on the Caribbean island of Barbados.

1816 CHINA The Chinese expel a British trade mission.

1817 LIBERIA The American Colonization Society begins to set up colonies in Liberia, Africa.

Economy of slavery

If slavery was abolished, many Southerners would lose a huge amount of money. Many planters had invested in both slaves and the land for the plantations. By 1860, the South had nearly four million slaves out of a population of nine million. Many Southerners were not very comfortable with the morals behind slavery. But even they could not imagine how much it would devastate the economy in the South if slavery was abolished.

Slavery in law

The law was a little confused in regard to how to treat slaves. On the one hand a slave was legally the property of his owner, just as a horse or table was. But on the other hand, slaves were clearly also human beings, no matter how "inferior" they might be thought to be. Laws laid out how slave owners should treat their slaves in a humane way.

These two attitudes toward slavery clearly contradicted one another. If a slave was only a piece of property, how could he or she be responsible for his or her actions? How could he or she be punished for a crime? In the end, the Southern courts could not resolve the contradiction. That would take a long war.

When war came in 1861, few soldiers on either side believed they were fighting for or against slavery.

THE DRED SCOTT DECISION

Dred Scott was a slave owned by a Missouri doctor, John Emerson. In 1834 Emerson took Scott to live in free territory for nine years. They returned to Missouri, where Emerson died in 1843. Scott and his wife took legal action to win their freedom on the grounds that Scott had once lived in free territory. The U.S. Supreme Court finally ruled on March 6, 1857, that freeing Scott would deprive Emerson's widow of her property. The decision effectively made slavery legal in all parts of the United States. The case caused outrage in the North and accelerated the war.

1818 WASHINGTON, D.C. The Stars and Stripes is adopted as the U.S. flag.

1818 NORTH AMERICA The 49th Parallel becomes the border between the United States and Canada.

1818 FLORIDA Spain cedes Florida to the United States.

1819 MISSOURI Missouri applies to enter the United States as a slave state.

1818 GREAT BRITAIN British writer Mary Shelley writes the classic Gothic novel *Frankenstein*.

1818 NEW ZEALAND The arrival of European settlers in New Zealand sparks a series of wars between different groups of the native Maori people.

1819 MALAYA The British found a trading station in Malaya that will become the port of Singapore.

Abolition Campaign

Opponents of slavery became more vocal in the 1830s. Supporters of abolition called for slavery to be outlawed throughout the United States. They brought the issue to the forefront of American politics.

The abolitionist Wendell Phillips speaks to an antislavery rally in Boston in 1851.

Slavery had existed in North America for 150 years longer than the United States itself—and opposition to slavery had existed just as long. Almost as soon as independence was declared during the Revolutionary War (1775–1783), some

1820–1822

UNITED STATES

c.1820 UNITED STATES
The Second Great Awakening begins; it will inspire many American Christians to turn against slavery.

1820 WASHINGTON, D.C. The Missouri Compromise allows Missouri to be admitted to the Union as a slave state, balanced by the creation of Maine as a free state. It helps keep the Union together for some 30 years.

OTHER EVENTS

1820 PACIFIC OCEAN
Christian missionaries arrive in Hawaii and Tonga.

1820 VIETNAM
The emperor of Vietnam remodels his capital city based on Chinese examples.

1820 LEBANON
American Christian missionaries arrive in Lebanon, but face strong resistance.

1821 MEXICO
Mexico declares its independence from Spain.

1820   1821

politicians argued that slavery should be forbidden in the new country. For most of the Founders who were shaping the new country, however, slavery was something to be tolerated. Thomas Jefferson, who became the third president of the United States, called it a "necessary evil," though he supported its gradual abolition. Jefferson himself owned slaves; so did other Founders, such as George Washington. There was a practical reason not to abolish slavery: No Southern state would join a union where slavery was banned.

Slavery had been abolished in all the states north of Maryland by 1804. Importing slaves was banned throughout the United States in 1807, although smuggling remained widespread until the 1860s.

Defending slavery

In the early 1800s slavery became more profitable. There was a worldwide demand for the cotton grown on Southern plantations. Cotton growing—and slavery—actually spread in the South. Supporters of slavery began to argue that it was a "positive good": for the economy, for society, even for the slaves themselves. It was now highly unlikely that gradual abolition would succeed. Opponents of slavery began a campaign that called for the immediate legal abolition of slavery.

Abolitionist tactics

The abolitionist campaign set out to win support for the cause. They published books and pamphlets and held lectures about the evils of slavery. One of the leading writers and speakers

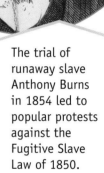

The trial of runaway slave Anthony Burns in 1854 led to popular protests against the Fugitive Slave Law of 1850.

1822 SOUTH CAROLINA Denmark Vesey is hanged for planning a slave revolt.

1822 OHIO Future Union general Ulysses S. Grant is born at Point Pleasant, Ohio.

1821 GREAT BRITAIN British scientist Michael Faraday invents the electric motor and generator.

1822 LIBERIA The first freed slaves from the United States arrive to found the city of Monrovia in present-day Liberia, West Africa.

1822 BRAZIL Brazil achieves independence from Spain.

A MORAL PERFECTIONISM

In 1831, William Lloyd Garrison published *The Liberator*, a newspaper devoted to ending slavery. In 1833, he and others founded the American Anti-Slavery Society, which spread throughout the North. They were influenced by a religious movement called the Second Great Awakening. It preached a doctrine of perfectionism that required Christians to work to end evils such as slavery. The abolitionists argued that slaveholders should repent of their sins by voluntarily freeing their slaves.

Campaigner William Lloyd Garrison led calls for the North to secede from the Union.

was Frederick Douglass. He was a former slave who wrote an autobiography in 1845. Other African Americans also played a prominent role in the campaign.

The political campaign

Some abolitionists believed that political power was the best way to end slavery. Members of Congress, such as Charles Sumner and Thaddeus Stevens, opposed legislation like the Fugitive Slave Law of 1850. The law let slave owners reclaim slaves who had run away, even if they were now in free states and territories. A new group emerged called the Free Soilers, who opposed the spread of slavery. They set up the Free Soil Party in 1848. The party was small, but it was powerful enough to put the antislavery issue at the heart of U.S. politics. The Free Soilers and other groups with similar beliefs created the Republican Party in 1854.

Turning to violence

By now, some abolitionists were considering violence, in the shape of a slave rebellion or a civil war. In 1856 John Brown, a fanatical abolitionist, led a gang that murdered five proslavery settlers in Kansas. In 1859, they seized a federal arsenal at Harpers Ferry, Virginia. Brown planned to give weapons to slaves to start a rebellion. He was soon captured, tried, and executed. John Brown became a powerful symbol for abolitionists, and his actions hastened the coming of the Civil War.

1823–1826

UNITED STATES

1823 WASHINGTON, D.C. The Monroe Doctrine warns against European interference in American affairs.

1824 NEW YORK Future Confederate president Jefferson Davis enrols in the U.S. Military Academy at West Point.

1824 WASHINGTON, D.C. The U.S. War Department sets up the Bureau of Indian Affairs.

OTHER EVENTS

1823 WEST AFRICA In West Africa, the Ashanti Kingdom goes to war with the British.

1824 MEXICO Mexico becomes a republic, three years after first declaring independence from Spain.

1823

1824

The triumph of abolition

Civil war finally came after the presidential election of 1860 sent the Republican Abraham Lincoln to the White House. Lincoln opposed slavery, so abolitionists believed that their chance had come. But Lincoln himself did not want to act too hastily, even after the Civil War began. He knew that abolition might have severe political consequences.

It was not until after over a year of fighting, in September 1862, that Lincoln issued the Emancipation Proclamation. Beginning January 1, 1863, slaves in the rebel states would be set free. In fact, most slaves had to wait for emancipation until 1865, after the defeat of the South. The Thirteenth Amendment to the Constitution abolished slavery in the United States.

Some historians say that Union armies and Free Soilers in Congress did far more to destroy slavery than the abolitionists did. However, abolitionists helped force people to think about the morals of slavery. They may have helped Northerners see the Civil War not as a conflict to prevent secession but as a struggle for human freedom.

Slaves provided free labor and meant the prewar South was slow to embrace new technologies.

AN INFLUENTIAL BOOK

In 1852, the abolitionist Harriet Beecher Stowe published *Uncle Tom's Cabin*. The novel told the story of Tom, a slave, and explained how badly he was treated. The description of the horrors of slavery was a huge success. It sold 50,000 copies in only two months, and became the bestselling novel of the 19th century. The book was criticized in the South, but in the North and in Europe it helped win more support for abolition. Abraham Lincoln later described Harriet Beecher Stowe as "the little lady who wrote the book that made this great war."

1825 NEW YORK The new Erie Canal completes a 363-mile (585km) waterway linking the Great Lakes to the Atlantic Ocean.

1825 NEW YORK Future Confederate commander Robert E. Lee enters West Point.

1825 GREAT BRITAIN The world's first railroad opens; it runs between Stockton and Darlington in northern England.

1826 BRAZIL The Brazilian emperor Dom Pedro signs a treaty with the British; its terms say that he must end the slave trade by 1851.

1826 FRANCE A French inventor takes the world's first permanent photograph.

The Missouri Compromise

When the debate came to a head in 1820, Congress avoided making a decision between slavery or abolition. The compromise they came up with helped avoid war for over 40 years.

Kentucky politician Henry Clay was largely responsible for the 1820 Missouri Compromise.

In 1819, slavery threatened to become a major issue. The territory of Missouri, where some settlers owned slaves, applied for statehood. That could have serious results far more widely than in Missouri. At the time, the United States had

1827–1829

UNITED STATES

1827 NEW YORK Joseph Smith, Jr, claims to be given *The Book of Mormon* by the angel Moroni in a vision; he founds the Church of Jesus Christ of Latter Day Saints.

1828 MARYLAND Work begins to construct the Baltimore & Ohio Railroad, the first steam-powered railroad in the United States.

OTHER EVENTS

1827 GREECE At the Battle of Navarino, the Ottoman navy is destroyed by a combined British, French, and Russian fleet.

1827   1828

equal numbers of free and slave states. The U.S. Senate was also evenly balanced. If Missouri joined, the balance would be upset.

A political balance

At first, the House of Representatives agreed to admit Missouri—but as a free state. After Southerners in the Senate blocked the proposal, Speaker of the House Henry Clay set out a compromise. He proposed that Missouri would join the Union as a slave state, as Southerners wished. But a new free state, Maine, would be created in north Massachusetts. That would keep the balance of power in the Senate. In the hopes of avoiding future problems, Jesse B. Thomas, an Illinois senator, proposed that a line be drawn along the latitude of 36° 30' (the southern border of Missouri). All states north of the line would be free—except Missouri—and all states to the south would permit slavery. New states would enter the Union in pairs, one free and one slave. The compromise and Thomas's amendment passed, and Missouri joined the Union in 1821.

This illustration from 1852 hails the men behind a new compromise in 1850. In the front row, from left to right, are Winfield Scott, Lewis Cass, Henry Clay, John Calhoun, Daniel Webster, and Millard Fillmore.

Delaying conflict

After the Mexican War ended in 1848, slavery again became an issue. A compromise in 1850 temporarily averted splitting the country, but the Kansas–Nebraska Act of 1854 effectively repealed the Missouri Compromise. The time was coming when the issue could no longer be compromised away.

1829 NEW YORK Robert E. Lee graduates West Point second in his class.

1829 INDIA In India, the British outlaw the Hindu tradition that a widow is burned to death on her husband's funeral pyre.

1829 GREECE The Ottoman Empire recognizes that the Greeks have the right to govern themselves.

Kansas—Nebraska Act

The Kansas—Nebraska Act of May 1854 allowed settlers
in the new U.S. territories to decide if they would permit slavery.
It was a major step toward the coming of war.

A cover for an anti-slavery song shows the burning of the Free State Hotel in Lawrence, Kansas.

The issue began with ambitions to build a transcontinental railroad between Chicago and California. In 1853 Stephen A. Douglas, a Democrat senator from Illinois, proposed the organization of a new territory. He hoped that the creation of

1830–1832

UNITED STATES

1830 WASHINGTON, D.C. The Indian Removal Act authorizes the government to resettle the five Native American tribes living east of the Mississippi River to territory set aside in the West.

1831 VIRGINIA Nat Turner leads a slave revolt in Southampton, Virginia, that leaves 55 whites dead.

OTHER EVENTS

1830 FRANCE A popular revolt in France forces King Charles X to abdicate; he is replaced by the Duke of Orléans, who takes the name Louis Philippe.

1830 BELGIUM Belgium breaks away from the Netherlands and proclaims its independence.

1831 WEST INDIES A slave uprising in Jamaica in the Caribbean hastens the end of slavery there.

1830   1831

Nebraska would be the first step in building the railroad. Southern politicians preferred a southern route for the railroad. They blocked the bill. Instead, Douglas came up with a plan to create two new territories: Nebraska and Kansas. The bill allowed settlers in the two territories to decide whether to allow slavery. Most people assumed that Nebraska would vote against slavery, while Kansas would vote for it.

Continuing opposition

Congress narrowly passed Douglas's bill in May 1854. Opponents of slavery were furious; the new act potentially permitted slavery in the North. It effectively undid the Missouri Compromise that for 30 years had kept the balance of power between North and South. The unpopularity in the North of both the act and the Democrats who supported it was clear in the congressional elections of fall 1854. The number of northern Democrats in the House of Representatives fell from 92 to 23, while opponents of the act elected 150 congressmen.

By 1856 opponents of the act had come together to form the new Republican Party. The act continued to provide a rallying point for antislavery forces. Eventually it led to the triumph of Republican Abraham Lincoln in the presidential elections of 1860, which in turn brought on secession and the Civil War.

In Kansas, the act resulted in years of violence, a period known as "Bleeding Kansas." Kansas was finally admitted to the Union as a free state in 1861.

This anti-slavery poster shows a young man getting ready to fight to stop slaves being thrown into the state of Kansas.

1831 MASSACHUSETTS
Bostonian William Lloyd Garrison begins publishing *The Liberator*, a newspaper devoted to ending slavery.

1831 THE SOUTH
The Underground Railroad for escaping slaves gets its name.

1832 SOUTH CAROLINA
John C. Calhoun of South Carolina promotes the idea that a state can nullify federal laws with which it disagrees.

1831 EGYPT The viceroy of Egypt, Muhammad Ali, begins a revolt against the Ottoman Empire.

1832 GREAT BRITAIN The size of the British electorate is doubled when the Great Reform Act gives the vote to well-off men.

1832 ALGERIA The Algerians begin a resistance campaign against French occupation.

An Abolitionist Martyr

John Brown was a religious fanatic. He hated slavery so much that he turned to violence to try to end it. When he was executed for his crimes, he became a martyr for the abolitionist cause.

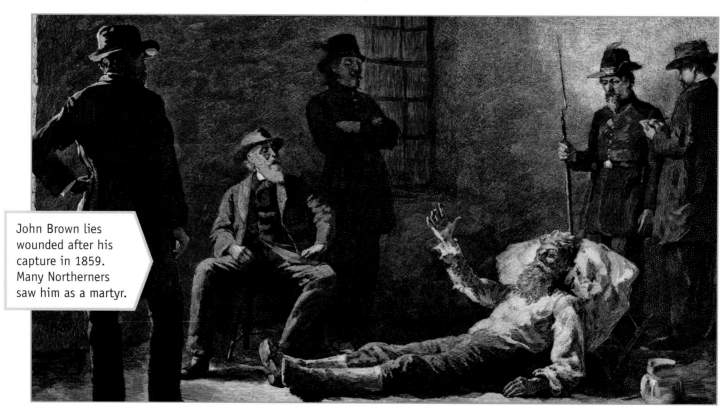

John Brown lies wounded after his capture in 1859. Many Northerners saw him as a martyr.

John Brown (1800–1859) had worked to improve the lives of black Americans for many years. He believed that both racism and slavery were sinful and had no place in the United States. He himself had lived for two years in a community of

1833–1835

UNITED STATES

1833 MASSACHUSETTS
The abolitionist William Lloyd Garrison founds the American Anti-Slavery Society.

1833 THE WEST Invention of the mechanical reaper, which encourages the growth of farming in the western United States.

OTHER EVENTS

1833 GREAT BRITAIN
A campaign by MP William Wilberforce results in a law that will abolish slavery in the British empire.

1833 EGYPT/SYRIA
Turkey recognizes the independence of Egypt and gives up control of Syria to Muhammad Ali.

1834 GREAT BRITAIN
Slavery is abolished throughout the British empire on January 1.

1833

1834

free blacks in New York State. He also acted as a "conductor" on the Underground Railroad: he provided a safe house for Southern slaves to use as they secretly escaped to the North.

After the Kansas–Nebraska Act came into law, Brown decided to take direct action. In 1855, he moved to Kansas with five of his sons. He aimed to help stop the territory from becoming a slave state. In 1856, proslavery settlers attacked the free-state community of Lawrence. Brown reacted violently. He and his gang killed five proslavery men on a raid on a settlement at Pottawatomie Creek.

The murders made Brown a hero for some abolitionists, but proslavers hated him and burned him out of his farm. With money from Northern abolitionists, he launched raids on plantations in neighboring Missouri, another slave state.

A failed raid

On October 16, 1859, Brown led a raid on Harpers Ferry, Virginia, where he seized the federal armory. He planned to pass weapons to slaves to spark a rebellion across the South. Instead, Brown and his men were trapped by U.S. forces. On October 18, U.S. Marines led by Colonel Robert E. Lee attacked the raiders. Ten of Brown's men were killed; Brown himself was wounded and captured, along with six others.

The authorities acted quickly to avoid tension between the pro- and antislavery sides. Brown was convicted of murder and treason. He was hanged on December 2, 1859.

Troops of the Fifty-Fifth Massachusetts Colored Regiment sing "John Brown's Body" as they march in Charleston, South Carolina in 1865. John Brown was a hero for the antislavery cause.

1835 CONNECTICUT Inventor Samuel Colt patents his revolving-breech pistol, known as the revolver.

1834 WEST INDIES About 700,000 slaves are emancipated in Britain's Caribbean colonies.

1835 SOUTH AFRICA In southern Africa 10,000 Dutch settlers (Boers) trek north inland in protest at the abolition of slavery in Britain's Cape Colony.

1835 INDIA The British dictate that children will be taught in English in areas of India under British control.

A New President

The election of the 16th president started the process of secession that led to the Civil War; Abraham Lincoln came to the White House determined that the Union would survive.

This photograph of President Abraham Lincoln was taken by Mathew Brady in 1864.

Lincoln's election and his presidency were both controversial. He was widely disliked in the South because he was known to be against slavery. In the North, he was criticized for abusing his powers as president. Despite the criticism, his skilled

1836–1838

UNITED STATES

1836 PHILADELPHIA Angelina Grimké writes her famous essay against slavery, "Appeal to the Christian Women of the United States."

1836 TEXAS Texas wins independence from Mexico.

OTHER EVENTS

1836 GREAT BRITAIN The Chartists in Britain are one of the first organized movements representing the demands of working people.

1836 BOLIVIA/PERU Bolivia and Peru form a united federation; it only lasts three years.

1837 CANADA Revolts break out against British rule in both Upper and Lower Canada.

1836

1837

leadership during the war fulfilled his aim of keeping the Union together. In doing so, he proved himself one of the most exceptional of all American leaders.

Early life

Abraham Lincoln had been born to a poor frontier family in a one-room log cabin in Kentucky on February 12, 1809. The family could not afford to send Lincoln to school, so he borrowed books to educate himself and joined a local debating society.

From 1834, Lincoln served four terms on the Illinois legislature as a member of the Whig Party. He studied law and became a successful lawyer in the state capital, Springfield. In 1846, he was elected to the U.S. House of Representatives.

Like other opponents of slavery, Lincoln was infuriated by the Kansas–Nebraska Act of 1854. He joined the Republican Party, which was created to oppose the expansion of slavery. In 1858, he became a member of the U.S. Senate. Two years later, the Republicans made Lincoln their candidate for president. In the election, he received 39.8 percent of the popular vote, but 180 of the 303 electoral college votes.

A color print from a photograph by Mathew Brady showing Lincoln reading to his youngest son.

Taking the nation to war

Not a single electoral college vote for Lincoln came from the slaveholding states of the South. When he took office in March 1861, seven Southern states had already left the Union. When the Confederacy demanded the surrender of Union forts in the

1838 THE SOUTH The "Trail of Tears": the U.S. Government forces native peoples, including the Cherokee, Creek, and Seminole, to move west.

1837 GREAT BRITAIN Victoria comes to the British throne, beginning a reign that will last 64 years and give its name to the Victorian Age.

1838 SIERRA LEONE When Britain's antislavery law comes into force, thousands of freed African slaves in Sierra Leone begin to head south to their former homelands.

1838 SOUTH AFRICA Boer settlers in Natal in southern Africa defeat a Zulu army that resists them in the Battle of Blood River.

An illustrated print of the Emancipation Proclamation of 1863.

South, Lincoln refused. In April, Confederate forces attacked Fort Sumter, South Carolina. Congress was not in session, but Lincoln made the decision to go to war. He effectively ran the war alone until Congress met on July 4. His opponents said he was acting like a dictator. The accusation was often repeated throughout his presidency.

A military commander

The Union strategy at the start of the war was based on the "Anaconda Plan" devised by General Winfield Scott. The plan aimed to use a naval blockade to prevent all trade in and out of the South, forcing the Confederacy to surrender. Lincoln approved the creation of the blockade, but he also ordered a number of military invasions of Southern territory. Throughout his time as commander-in-chief, Lincoln listened to his generals but made his own decisions.

Over the course of the war, Lincoln proved one of the best commanders-in-chief in American history. According to some historians, Lincoln may even have been helped by the fact that he had no military experience. At a time of unprecedentedly large armies and deadly modern weapons, traditional military thinking was of little use. Lacking formal training, Lincoln applied his intelligence and often came up with strategies that contradicted the military textbooks.

One result of Lincoln's ideas about the war was conflict with his generals. In September 1862, the popular general George B. McClellan failed to pursue the retreating Confederates after

LINCOLN'S APPOINTEES

Lincoln was good at choosing excellent people for important jobs, even overlooking his personal feelings. He selected men to serve in his cabinet who he did not necessarily agree with. Lincoln also showed faith in the Union military commander Ulysses S. Grant, who many people criticized as a drunkard.

1839–1841

UNITED STATES

1839 VIRGINIA The Virginia Military Institute (VMI) is established at the state arsenal at Lexington, Virginia.

1840 NEW YORK Future Union commander William T. Sherman joins the U.S. Army.

OTHER EVENTS

1839 ATLANTIC OCEAN The first ship to cross the Atlantic Ocean using only steam power, the *Sirius*, arrives in New York from London.

1839 TURKEY A new sultan, Abdul Mejid, begins a program of reforms in the Ottoman Empire.

1840 GREAT BRITAIN The world's first postage stamp—the Penny Black—comes into use in Britain.

1839   1840

the Union victory at Antietam (Sharpsburg). Lincoln removed McClellan from command of the Army of the Potomac. The president was determined to find commanders who would be more aggressive. Lincoln went on to fire several more generals he thought were too timid.

Short-lived triumph

The first years of the war were difficult for the Union, but Lincoln held the cause together. In November 1864, after a series of Union military successes, he was easily reelected for a second term as president. On April 9, 1865, news arrived of the surrender of Confederate General Robert E. Lee.

In his second inaugural address, Lincoln set out his ideas about how to bring the seceded states back into the Union after the war ended. He argued that the process of reconstruction should be carried out "with malice toward none, and charity for all."

In the end, the task of reconstruction was left for others. On April 14, Lincoln was shot by John Wilkes Booth at Ford's Theater in Washington, D.C. He died the next day.

This engraving shows the ceremony of Lincoln's second inauguration on March 4, 1865.

LINCOLN THE POLITICIAN

Lincoln was the first president of the new Republican Party. His cabinet included former Whigs and Democrats and he appointed men of all backgrounds to lead the Union army. Lincoln's critics said he trampled on the U.S. Constitution. He argued that it was worth sacrificing one-tenth of it to save the other nine-tenths. He pioneered the presidential use of executive orders, or laws that were not discussed by Congress. His executive orders included the Emancipation Proclamation of 1863.

1841 MASSACHUSETTS Former slave Frederick Douglass addresses an antislavery meeting, becoming a leading figure of the Abolition movement.

1840 CANADA The British governors of Canada plan to unite Upper and Lower Canada into a single country.

1841 BORNEO A British aristocrat, Sir James Brooke, becomes ruler of Sarawak in Borneo.

1841 TURKEY European powers agree to forbid warships from passing through the Dardanelles between the Mediterranean and the Black Sea.

Election of Abraham Lincoln

Lincoln was the Republican Party candidate in the 1860 presidential election. He defeated a Democratic Party deeply split over the issue of slavery. Lincoln's victory would had dramatic consequences.

In Charleston, South Carolina, a crowd greets the news of Lincoln's election with a cold silence.

The Republican Party had been formed in 1854, in the aftermath of the Kansas–Nebraska Act of the same year. Republicans opposed any further expansion of slavery into the new western territories of the United States.

1842–1844

UNITED STATES

1842 GEORGIA
U.S. surgeon William Crawford Long performs the first operation using ether as an anesthetic.

1843 MASSACHUSETTS
Massachusetts legalizes interracial marriage.

OTHER EVENTS

1842 CHINA The British defeat the Chinese in the First Opium War, and force China to grant them trading privileges and to hand them Hong Kong.

1842 AFGHANISTAN The British are defeated in Afghanistan; of the 16,000 men who invaded the country four years earlier, only 12 survive.

1843 INDIA At the Battle of Hyderabad, the British East India Company conquers the states of Punjab and Sind.

1842

1843

A divided opposition

The Republicans nominated Lincoln as their candidate for president in 1860. His running mate was Hannibal Hamlin of Maine. Meanwhile, their opponents were fighting among themselves. The Democratic National Convention was held on April 23, 1860, in Charleston, South Carolina. It became clear that the party was split into two opposed groups. With such a divided party, neither group seemed to have much chance of winning the election.

The election's aftermath

In the election of November 6, 1860, Lincoln only won 39.8 percent of the popular vote. He was victorious, however, because he won 180 votes in the electoral college.

This cartoon shows Lincoln and Northern Democrat Stephen Douglas in a race to reach the White House.

It can't stop me for I built it

You find me in dis yer Fence Massa Daglis.

How can I get over this Rail Fence.

The South reacted quickly. On December 20, 1860, South Carolina voted 159 to 0 to leave the Union. It was soon followed by six other Southern states. Delegates from the seceded states met at Montgomery, Alabama, on February 4, 1861. On February 8, the convention adopted a constitution for a new nation, the Confederate States of America. The next day, it elected Jefferson Davis as the provisional president.

Davis took up his position as Confederate president two weeks before Lincoln, whose inauguration took place on March 4, 1861. Only a month later, on April 12, 1861, the war began when Confederates fired on Fort Sumter in South Carolina.

1843 NEW YORK Future Union commander Ulysses S. Grant graduates from the Military Academy at West Point.

1844 WASHINGTON, D.C. The United States forces China to grant it privileged trading status.

1844 WASHINGTON, D.C. The inventor Samuel Morse sends the first telegraph message, from Washington, D.C., to Baltimore.

1843 WEST AFRICA The British establish a colony in Gambia in West Africa.

1844 HAITI The Dominican Republic declares its independence from Haiti on the island of Santo Domingo.

States' Rights

Many people in the South believed that the federal government did not have the right to interfere with certain areas of state affairs. They saw the Civil War as a defense of states' rights.

Georgians at a public meeting in Savannah on November 8, 1860, demand secession.

Since the Declaration of Independence of 1776, Americans had debated the balance of power between the national government and the individual states. People who supported states' rights argued that the states had chosen to give some

1845–1847

UNITED STATES

1845 MASSACHUSETTS
Former slave Frederick Douglass publishes his autobiography.

1845 TEXAS
The United States annexes Texas.

1845 MISSISSIPPI
Future Confederate president Jefferson Davis is elected to Congress as a Democrat.

1846 MISSOURI
The slave Dred Scott goes to court to claim his freedom.

OTHER EVENTS

1845 IRELAND The potato harvest fails; the resulting famine causes the deaths of a million people.

1846 OREGON The Oregon Treaty divides the Pacific Northwest between the United States and Canada at the 49th Parallel.

1845   1846

powers to the Union, but were still in charge of most of their own affairs. The debate grew more heated in the 1850s. People in the South feared more federal interference with the rights of the states: and most of all with the right to preserve slavery.

The Constitution did not really discuss slavery. It left nearly all questions about the subject to the states themselves. But the Constitution was less clear about whether slavery should be allowed in new territories as the nation expanded.

The regimental flag of the 3rd Florida Infantry had a motto that summed up the mood in the Confederacy.

A changing argument

President Jefferson Davis and other Confederate leaders did not want to be seen as fighting simply to preserve slavery. They used states' rights to defend the secession of the Southern states. It was only after the war, however, that states' rights became a more important justification for the conflict. As time passed, even many Southerners came to see slavery as being morally indefensible. People in the South increasingly argued that the war had been about states' rights, not about slavery. But while states' rights did help bring about secession, the only right that most Southerners cared about at the time was the right to protect slavery. Others, such as the right to set taxes, would never have caused civil war.

1846 MEXICO The Mexican–American War breaks out.

1846 ILLINOIS Illinois lawyer Abraham Lincoln is elected to the House of Representatives.

1847 MEXICO Future Confederate commander Robert E. Lee is promoted to the rank of brevet major in the U.S. Army.

1847 IRELAND A famine drives more than 200,000 people to emigrate in that year, mainly to North America.

1847 LIBERIA Liberia, a state set up as a home for freed slaves, becomes independent.

The South Leaves the Union

When the United States was created, the Founders had intended the Union to be permanent. Yet between December 1860 and June 1861, eleven Southern states decided to leave the United States.

This Northern cartoon from January 1861 attacks the secession of South Carolina and Georgia.

The U.S. Constitution had not even mentioned the right of a state to leave the Union. But to the supporters of secession, as the process of leaving was known, it was obvious that the right existed. The states had voluntarily chosen to enter the

1848–1850

UNITED STATES

1848 CALIFORNIA The California Gold Rush inspires a wave of settlers to the West Coast.

1848 THE SOUTHWEST The Mexican War ends with the United States gaining all Mexican land north of the Rio Grande.

1848 NEW YORK Antislavery supporters form the Free Soil Party.

1849 ILLINOIS Abraham Lincoln retires from politics to practice law.

OTHER EVENTS

1848 EUROPE Prodemocracy uprisings take place in many countries, including Italy, France, Germany, Austria, and Hungary.

1848 GERMANY The *Communist Manifesto* is published by Karl Marx and Friedrich Engels, German revolutionary thinkers.

1849 WEST AFRICA The French found Libreville in Gabon, Africa, as a home for freed slaves.

1848

1849

Union, they argued. Therefore it was clear that they could also choose to leave—especially if the federal government was abusing its power. According to this view, the states who had joined the Union had voluntarily delegated only some of their powers to the federal government. Sovereignty, or ultimate authority, still belonged to the individual states.

Threat to the South

Secession became an important political issue in the South in the second half of the 1850s. In the North, the Republican Party was founded in 1854 to oppose the expansion of slavery. During the campaign for the 1860 presidential election, the Republicans tried to calm Southern fears. They promised that they would not abolish slavery in states where it already existed. But they made it clear that they would keep slavery out of any new states that joined the Union. In the eyes of many Southerners, this would eventually tip the balance in Congress and in the courts in favor of the free states. It could therefore lead to the abolition of slavery in the future. Even moderate Southerners began to consider secession.

The Deep South secedes

The Republican candidate Abraham Lincoln was elected as president in November 1860. Almost at once, the seven states of the Deep South—the southernmost states, where plantation agriculture was most common—began to secede. South Carolina voted to leave the Union on December 20, 1860. It was followed over the next two months by Mississippi, Florida,

Senator John C. Calhoun was the most prominent supporter of secession before the war.

1849 MARYLAND Harriet Tubman escapes from slavery; she later leads more than 300 slaves to freedom on the "Underground Railroad."

1850 CALIFORNIA California joins the United States as the 31st state.

1850 WASHINGTON, D.C. The Fugitive Slave Act requires all states to return slaves to their former masters, increasing tension between the northern and southern states.

1850 NEW YORK The first Chinese emigrants arrive in the United States, where they settle in New York City.

1850 CHINA The Taiping Rebellion breaks out in southern China; the uprising against the Qing (Manchu) Dynasty will continue for 14 years.

1850 EAST AFRICA Tippu Tib, a Zanzibari merchant, creates a personal empire in the eastern Congo region in East Africa.

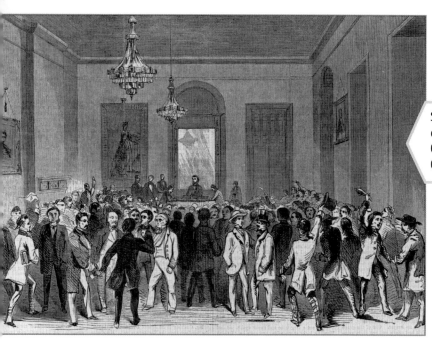

Southern Democrats debate secession in Charleston, South Carolina, in April 1860.

Alabama, Georgia, Louisiana, and Texas. In February, representatives from the seceding states met to create a country, the Confederate States of America.

Only the seven states of the Deep South intially seceded. If the Confederacy was going to be able to maintain its independence, it was vital that the remaining eight slave states joined them.

Those states, known as the Upper South, were the slave states closest to the North. Their citizens were in favor of slavery, but they hesitated to leave the Union. If war came, they would become battlefields. There were also large parts of North Carolina, Virginia, and Tennessee where there were few plantations and few slaveholders. People in those areas tended to be strongly in favor of remaining in the Union.

COOPERATIONISTS

In fall 1860, many people in the Upper South states were "cooperationists." Their name came because they favored collective action among the Southern states inside the Union. Even after the secession of the Deep South states, many cooperationists waited to see what Lincoln would do in office. They still thought they might be able to work with him.

Fight for the forts

On March 4, 1861, Lincoln was inaugurated as president. He repeated that he did not intend to change slavery where it existed. But he also sent a warning to the Confederacy. The federal government was determined to retain control of Union properties in the South. Attention soon focused on the Union-held Fort Sumter, in Charleston Harbor, South Carolina. Confederates opened fire on the fort on April 12, 1861. The

1851–1853

UNITED STATES

1851 NEW YORK U.S. inventor Isaac Singer invents the first continuous-stitch sewing machine.

1852 MAINE Harriet Beecher Stowe publishes the antislavery novel *Uncle Tom's Cabin*.

OTHER EVENTS

1851 NIGERIA The British lay siege to Lagos in Nigeria to end the extensive slave trading there.

1851 AUSTRALIA The discovery of gold near Bathurst in New South Wales begins a gold rush in Australia.

1852 NEW ZEALAND Britain's colony in New Zealand gains a formal constitution.

1851   1852

Union troops in the fort surrendered two days later. The next day, April 15, Lincoln called 75,000 state militia troops into federal service. He was ready to fight.

Second wave of secession

Fort Sumter sparked a wave of secession in the states of the Upper South. The most important was Virginia, which seceded on April 17. Virginia had modern industry and the largest population in the South. It lay directly across the Potomac River from Washington, D.C. It was also home to outstanding military commanders, including Robert E. Lee and Thomas J. Jackson. Arkansas, North Carolina, and Tennessee followed Virginia. Four slave states—Delaware, Kentucky, Maryland, and Missouri—stayed in the Union.

The South had founded a nation on a belief in states' rights. As the war went on, however, the states failed to give the government the power it needed. In the end, secession helped bring about the fall of the nation it had created.

An engraving in *Frank Leslie's Illustrated Newspaper* shows a secession meeting in Charleston, South Carolina.

SENATOR JOHN C. CALHOUN

In 1832, South Carolina Senator John C. Calhoun (1782–1850) persuaded his state to adopt the idea that a state could nullify, or cancel, a federal law with which it disagreed. South Carolina nullified a set of federal tariffs and declared itself ready to leave the Union if the government in Washington tried to collect the tax. After President Andrew Jackson threatened South Carolina with military force, the crisis subsided. By the 1840s, Calhoun was advocating secession if Congress passed antislavery legislation. Calhoun died in 1850.

1852 NEW YORK The nativist, anti-immigrant "Know-Nothing" Party is founded.

1853 MISSOURI The Missouri Supreme Court refuses to grant Dred Scott his freedom; he appeals against the decision to the U.S. Supreme Court.

1853 RHODE ISLAND Future Civil War general Ambrose Burnside patents the Burnside carbine.

1853 CALIFORNIA Future Union commander William T. Sherman quits the U.S. Army to manage a San Francisco bank.

1852 SOUTH AFRICA In southern Africa, Boer settlers found the republic of Transvaal, northeast of Cape Colony.

1853 JAPAN U.S. Commodore Matthew Perry arrives in Japan with a fleet of "black ships," and forces Japan into agreeing a trade agreement.

The First Shots

Fort Sumter in Charleston Harbor, South Carolina, was a minor Union outpost. On April 12, 1861, it gained lasting fame as the location where the first shots of the Civil War were fired.

Confederate cannons open fire on Fort Sumter, marking the beginning of the Civil War.

Abraham Lincoln had warned the South in his inauguration speech that the government intended to remain in control of Union properties in the Confederacy. In particular, there were a number of Union forts in what was now Confederate

1854–1856

UNITED STATES

1854 KANSAS The Kansas–Nebraska Act destroys the 1820 Missouri Compromise over slavery; bitter fighting breaks out in "Bloody Kansas."

1854 MICHIGAN Free Soilers combine with others to form the Republican Party.

1855 NEW YORK William J. Hardee publishes *Rifle and Light Infantry Tactics* (*Hardee's Tactics*), the standard drill manual used by both sides in the Civil War.

OTHER EVENTS

1854 RUSSIA The Crimean War breaks out; Britain and France go to war as allies of Turkey after Russia expands around the Black Sea.

1855 RUSSIA Pioneering British nurse Florence Nightingale cares for wounded soldiers in the Crimean War.

1854   1855

territory. One was Fort Sumter. It was occupied by a small Union force commanded by Major Robert Anderson. In March 1861, Anderson rejected attempts by the Confederate authorities to negotiate the peaceful evacuation of the fort. He believed that he was entitled to defend the fort as federal property.

The stand-off at Fort Sumter presented Confederate President Jefferson Davis with a problem. Now that the Confederacy had declared its independence, it was not possible to simply allow a Union garrison to remain in the heart of Confederate territory. On the other hand, South Carolina was home to some of the most militant secessionists. He did not want them to try to seize the fort on their own initiative.

A weak position

Anderson and his second-in-command, Captain Abner Doubleday, had only limited resources. The fort was only half-finished. The poorly-supplied garrison totaled 127 soldiers with only 66 cannons, some of which were not even mounted on carriages. The fort was so weak that Davis and his cabinet ordered General Pierre G.T. Beauregard to seize it before Union reinforcements could arrive.

Beauregard's troops set up artillery batteries around the edge of the harbor, on nearby forts, and on an ironclad ship. They gave Anderson a final chance to surrender at 3:20 A.M.

Confederate landowner Edmund Ruffin 1794–1865 is credited with firing the first shot on Fort Sumter.

1856 KANSAS John Brown and his followers murder five proslavery settlers at Pottawatomie Creek in Kansas.

1856 NEW YORK Albert J. Myer introduces the wigwag system of military signals.

1855 EGYPT Engineer Ferdinand de Lesseps is hired to build the Suez Canal to link the Mediterranean and Red Seas.

1856 RUSSIA The Crimean War ends in defeat for Russia.

1856 CHINA The Second Opium War: Britain goes to war to force China to allow the continued importation of opium into the country from India.

Fort Sumter has great symbolic importance as the location of the first clash of the war.

on April 12, when Confederate Colonel James Chesnut and Captain Stephen D. Lee rowed out to the fort. Anderson refused to surrender. He believed that new troops and supplies would reach him by sea.

Under fire

Chesnut and Lee left, warning Anderson that shelling would start within the hour. At 4:30 A.M. the first Confederate shell struck the fort. Anderson gave Abner Doubelday the honor of firing the Union's first shot in response, at around 7:00 A.M. The fort was so poorly supplied, however, that there was only enough ammunition to fire a few rounds now and then. Such infrequent fire had little effect on the enemy.

In contrast, the Confederates had plentiful ammunition for their artillery. Led by the battery at Point Cummings on Morris Island to the south, they subjected the fort to a heavy barrage that lasted until daybreak. By the time the guns fell silent, several fires had broken out inside the fort.

Later in the day, the Union supply ship Anderson had been expecting, *The Star of the West*, arrived at Charleston. The ship was unable to reach the garrison trapped inside the fort, however, as Confederate artillery fire prevented it from entering the harbor.

MAJOR ANDERSON

Robert Anderson was a former slave owner and staunch Kentuckian who nevertheless remained loyal to the Union. Anderson's decision to move his small garrison from Fort Moultrie to Fort Sumter forced the standoff that led to the start of the Civil War.

1857–1859

UNITED STATES

1857 WASHINGTON, D.C. The Supreme Court denies Dred Scott his freedom. The decision effectively makes the Missouri Compromise unconstitutional and increases tensions between North and South.

1857 WASHINGTON, D.C. Senator James Henry Hammond of South Carolina tells the U.S. Senate "No, you do not dare make war on cotton. No power on earth dares make war on it. Cotton is king."

OTHER EVENTS

1857 INDIA Indian troops in the British Army begin the Indian Mutiny.

1857 AFGHANISTAN Afghanistan becomes independent of Persia.

1857

The fall of the fort

The following night passed quietly, but as dawn broke on April 13, the Confederate batteries resumed their heavy shelling. A shell sparked another fire in the barracks inside the fort. As the smoke grew thicker, the Union troops had to lie on the ground in order to breathe. At 12:48 P.M. a shot hit the flagstaff, which fell down, taking the Stars and Stripes with it. Having seen the flag fall, Confederate Colonel Louis T. Wigfall rowed out to the fort. He demanded its surrender—and this time Anderson agreed. The first clash of the Civil War had ended in a Confederate victory. Its only casualty came during the surrender ceremony on April 14. During a 100-gun Union salute to the flag, the 50th gun exploded, killing one of its firing crew.

The Confederates occupied Fort Sumter for most of the war. It enabled them to ship supplies into Charleston, breaking the Union blockade. Union forces tried repeatedly to retake the fort. Confederates finally evacuated Fort Sumter on February 17, 1865, when Union troops entered South Carolina from Georgia.

A great patriotic rally was held in New York on April 20, 1861, a week after the shelling of Fort Sumter.

THE ATLANTIC HARBOR FORTS

Fort Sumter in Charleston Harbor was one of a number of similar fortifications that had been built to protect the Atlantic seaports of North America from foreign warships. They were among the newest and strongest forts in the country. Like Fort Pulaski, off Savannah, Georgia, Fort Sumter had walls 5 feet (1.5 m) thick. They were strong enough to withstand cannon fire from enemy ships. The forts' seacoast guns could themselves fire a 32-pound (14.5 kg) iron cannonball a distance of over 1 mile (1.6 km).

1858 ILLINOIS Abraham Lincoln, in his debates with Stephen Douglas in a race for the U.S. Senate, declares "A house divided against itself cannot stand."

1859 OREGON Oregon is admitted to the Union and becomes the 33rd state.

1859 VIRGINIA Abolitionist John Brown raids the armory at Harper's Ferry, intending to arm a slave revolt.

1858 INDIA The British government takes over the rule of India from the East India Company.

1859 GERMANY The German National Union is founded to campaign for a united Germany.

1859 VIETNAM The French begin to occupy Cochin China, later known as Vietnam.

Strangling the South

The Commanding General of the U.S. Army, Winfield Scott, devised the Anaconda Plan at the start of the war. The plan aimed to starve the South into submission.

This cartoon shows Winfield Scott's "Anaconda Plan" as a snake encircling the South.

Scott's strategy was based on the North's great advantage over the South in terms of resources. The North had more arms, more industry, more people, and more food. Scott argued that it would be possible to surround the Confederate states and

1860–1862

UNITED STATES

1860 WASHINGTON, D.C. Republican candidate Abraham Lincoln is elected as the 16th president of the United States.

1860 THE SOUTH South Carolina secedes from the Union; it will be followed by ten more states.

1860 THE SOUTH There are 3.5 million slaves in the South (up from 657,000 in 1790).

1861 THE SOUTH The secessionist states make plans to create their own country, the Confederate States of America.

OTHER EVENTS

1860 ITALY Nationalist Giuseppe Garibaldi and his "Thousand Redshirts" win control of Sicily and southern Italy, marking the beginning of Italian unification.

1860 AUSTRALIA Robert O'Hare Burke and William John Wills make the first overland crossing of Australia.

1860   1861

make it impossible for them to trade. As he outlined in May 1861 in a letter to another senior Union commander, Major General George B. McClellan, the shortage of supplies would eventually force the Confederacy to surrender.

Blockade at sea

To some extent, Scott's plan followed steps that were already underway. On April 19, President Lincoln had ordered the Union Navy to stop all naval traffic into or out of major Confederate ports. By the end of April, the blockade stretched from Norfolk, Virginia, around the coast to Galveston, Texas. Scott's plan would make this cordon even tighter. He aimed to shut down the Confederacy's Atlantic trade entirely.

This engraving shows the Fire Zouaves leaving for the front; the regiment was made up of New York firefighters.

The Mississippi River

In the West, Scott proposed that the Union could split the western parts of the Confederacy—Texas, Arkansas, and most of Louisiana—from the rest of the South. The key was gaining control of the Mississippi River. Confederates held the river from Tennessee south to the Gulf of Mexico. The Union's aim should therefore be to capture the forts in the Mississippi Delta and to occupy the port of New Orleans, which controlled the delta. Meanwhile, an army of 60,000 and a fleet of gunboats would sail downriver from Illinois. As Scott

1861 SOUTH CAROLINA
The first shots of the Civil War are fired at Fort Sumter; Confederates seize the stronghold in Charleston Harbor.

1861 VIRGINIA
Confederates win a decisive victory in the first large battle, Bull Run (or Manassas).

1862 TENNESSEE
Union forces win the Battle of Shiloh, taking control of the Mississippi River.

1862 MARYLAND
A Confederate invasion of the North is halted at the Battle of Antietam (Sharpsburg).

1862 LOUISIANA
Union forces capture New Orleans, the most important port in the South.

1862 INDIA Demand for cotton caused by the Civil War fuels an economic boom in India.

1862 PRUSSIA Otto von Bismarck becomes premier of Prussia; he will mastermind German unification.

Union artillery prepare for the Battle of Big Bethel, one of the earliest land battles of the war, on June 19, 1861.

explained, his strategy had the advantage that it would "envelop the insurgent States and bring them to terms with less bloodshed than by any other plan."

Two considerations

Two main considerations underlay Scott's plan. First, the Union Army was actually very small. He had a tiny force of 16,000 professional soldiers, or "regulars;" most of them were in the West. President Lincoln had called for 75,000 volunteers, but these militia were only enrolling for three months. They would be of little use in a long campaign. Lincoln had promised Scott an extra 25,000 regulars, plus 60,000 volunteers, who would enlist for three years. Scott was worried that this would still not be enough. Scott's other consideration was that he hoped to avoid the devastation of the South. As a Virginian himself, he was highly aware of the need to limit the war and its consequences as much as possible.

Public opinion

Scott's strategy was cautious and long term. It relied on squeezing the South economically rather than attacking it quickly on the battlefield. It was out of step with public opinion in the North. The press ridiculed the plan's caution. They

WINFIELD SCOTT

With a long and illustrious career, including leading U.S. forces in the Mexican War, Scott was almost 75 years old when he led the Union armies at the start of the Civil War. Although a Virginian, Scott had refused to join the Confederacy, instead pledging himself to the Union cause.

1863–1865

1863 WASHINGTON, D.C. The Emancipation Proclamation declares all slaves in rebel states to be free.

1863 PENNSYLVANIA The Battle of Gettysburg ends the Confederate invasion of the North.

1863 MISSISSIPPI The Union capture of Vicksburg splits the Confederacy in two.

1864 GEORGIA/CAROLINAS The March to the Sea. General William T. Sherman leads a Union army through Georgia and the Carolinas, causing great destruction.

1863 MEXICO French forces occupy Mexico City and proclaim Maximilian of Austria

1863 EGYPT The U.S. Civil War leads to a boom in cotton cultivation in Egypt.

1864 SWITZERLAND The International Red Cross is founded at Geneva, Switzerland.

1863   1864

called it "the Anaconda Plan" for a snake from South America that coils around its prey and squeezes it to death. The press, the public, politicians, and army officers were all eager for a quick victory. Despite Scott's warnings against acting too fast, the North was gripped with war fever. Northerners wanted to strike at the Confederate capital in Richmond, Virginia, barely 100 miles (160 km) from Washington.

In the face of such popular excitement, the Anaconda Plan was quietly dropped. Winfield himself retired from the army in November. He was replaced as commanding general by his junior officer, George McClellan. But the Union did adopt at least part of Scott's plan to regain the Mississippi River. The campaign began in February 1862 and continued in April with the recapture of New Orleans. It proved a long and bitter struggle, but played a vital part in the Union's eventual victory.

The Union mobilized and trained thousands of volunteers, like these infantry drilling in 1861.

PUBLIC OPINION IN THE NORTH

From the start of the war, the government in the North made great efforts to make sure the public supported the conflict. In New York, soldiers' aid and relief societies appeared. Churches and schools made and collected useful things for the troops. Voluntary efforts were coordinated by the United States Sanitary Commission. Many Northern women became involved. They were pleased to be able to make a contribution to the troops at the front.

In Boston, the North East Loyal Publications Society gathered up bits of pro-Union gossip and sent it out to small-town newspapers. Editors were happy to use the free copy and readers were happy to have their views confirmed.

1865 VIRGINIA Union forces capture the Confederate capital at Richmond, Virginia.

1865 VIRGINIA Confederate forces under Robert E. Lee surrender at Appomattox Court House.

1865 WASHINGTON, D.C. President Abraham Lincoln is assassinated a week after the Confederate surrender.

1864 FRANCE Louis Pasteur introduces the pasteurization process, which reduces harmful bacteria in milk.

1865 SOUTH AMERICA The bloodiest war in Latin American history, the War of the Triple Alliance, breaks out between Paraguay and Argentina, Brazil, and Uruguay.

1865 AUSTRIA Studies by the Austrian monk Gregor Mendel begin the modern science of genetics.

1865 RUSSIA Russian author Leo Tolstoy writes his great novel *War and Peace*.

NEED TO KNOW

Some of the subjects covered in this book feature in many state curricula. These are topics you should understand.

General causes of the war:
slavery
states' rights
expansion
politics

Political events:
Missouri Compromise 1820
Dred Scott Case
Kansas–Nebraska Act
Election of 1860

Anti-slavery campaigns:
Underground Railroad
Abolitionism
Uncle Tom's Cabin

KNOW THIS

This section summarizes the two major themes of this book: the causes of the war, and the role of slavery in U.S. history.

CAUSES

STATES' RIGHTS

The Southern states claimed to be fighting for the right to govern themselves. They argued that the U.S. Constitution only gave limited powers to the federal government. Most powers remained with the states. This was called states' rights.

SLAVERY

The main difference between the North and the South was their attitude toward slavery. In the North, slavery was illegal. In the South, slavery was the basis of the whole economy. Most Southerners believed that abolishing slavery would destroy their lifestyle.

EXPANSION

In the 19th century, the United States was expanding. It became important to decide whether new parts of the Union would allow slavery or not.

INDUSTRY

In the first half of the 19th century the North had become very industrialized. Its people lived in big cities and worked in factories. It had many mines, iron works, and railroads. The South was mainly an agricultural area. Its people lived in small towns, villages, and farms.

POLITICS

In the 1850s a new political party was founded. The Republican Party supported business and industry; it drew its support from the cities of the North. The South was dominated by the Democratic Party.

SLAVERY

- The first slaves arrived in North America in 1619.
- When the United States was created in 1776, the Declaration of Independence said that all men had a right to be free; but it did not include slaves.
- In the new country, a slave was counted as being equal to three-fifths of a U.S. citizen.
- The campaign against slavery was inspired by Christians such as Quakers.
- The Abolition movement began in the 1820s.
- Slavery was abolished in the North in the early 19th century.
- By the time of the Civil War, there were 3.9 million slaves in the United States.

TEST YOURSELF

These questions will help you discover what you have learned from this book.
Check the pages listed in the answers below.

1. **When did the first slaves arrive in North America?**

2. **What were the main crops grown by slaves in the South?**

3. **Who founded the anti-slavery newspaper *The Liberator*?**

4. **For how long did the Missouri Compromise solve the problems caused by slavery?**

5. **What did Abraham Lincoln call Harriet Beecher Stowe?**

6. **Why did Dred Scott argue that he should be freed?**

7. **When was the Republican Party founded?**

8. **How many electoral votes did Abraham Lincoln win in the South in the 1860 presidential election?**

9. **What was the first state to leave the Union?**

10. **Where were the first shots of the Civil War fired?**

ANSWERS

1. 1619, in Virginia Colony (see page 11). 2. Cotton, tobacco, rice (see page 7). 3. William Lloyd Garrison (see page 16). 4. For 34 years, until the Kansas–Nebraska Act in 1854 (see page 19). 5. "The little lady who wrote the book that made this big war" (see page 17). 6. Because he had once lived in free territory (see page 13). 7. 1854 (see page 28). 8. None (see page 25). 9. South Carolina (see page 33). 10. Fort Sumter, Charleston Harbor, South Carolina (see page 38).

GLOSSARY

abolition The ending of slavery; supporters of abolition were known as abolitionists.

arsenal A place where weapons and ammunition are stored.

batteries Groups of heavy guns, such as cannons.

blockade Measures aimed at preventing trade by using ships to intercept vessels heading toward port.

compromise A solution to a problem that takes a halfway path between two extreme positions.

Confederacy A league of members united by a common purpose; the word was used to describe the Southern side in the Civil War.

convention An assembly that meets to discuss what political ideas to follow.

cooperationist A Southerner who believed it was better to try to work with the government than to leave the Union.

dictator A politician who governs on his or her own, without consulting the rest of the government.

emancipation Another word for "freedom."

federal A word referring to the U.S. government in Washington, D.C.

garrison A group of soldiers who occupy a military post.

inauguration A ceremony held when a new president takes office.

militia Part of a country's army made up of citizens who are called on to serve in times of emergency.

plantation A large-scale agricultural estate; in the South, plantations were used to grow crops such as sugar, tobacco, cotton, and rice.

planter Someone who owns a plantation.

radical Someone who holds extreme views.

secession Breaking away from the Union; states that seceded from the Union formed the Confederacy.

Union The United States of America; the word described the Northern side in the Civil War.

FURTHER READING

BOOKS

Beller, Susan Provost. *Billy Yank and Johnny Reb: Soldiering in the Civil War.* Twenty-First Century Books, 2008.

Burgan, Michael. *Fort Sumter* (We the People). Compass Point Books, 2006.

Burgan, Michael. *The Battle of Gettysburg.* Capstone Press, 2006.

Doeden, Matt. *The Civil War: An Interactive History Adventure.* Capstone Press, 2010.

Lassieur, Allison. *The Underground Railroad: An Interactive History Adventure.* Capstone Press, 2008.

Mattern, Joanne. *The Big Book of the Civil War: Fascinating Facts about the Civil War, Including Historic Photographs, Maps and Documents.* Courage Books, 2007.

Miller, Reagan. *A Nation Divided: Causes of the Civil War* (Understanding the Civil War). Crabtree Publishing Company, 2011.

Mountjoy, Shane. *Causes of the Civil War: The Differences Between the North and South.* Chelsea House Publishers, 2009.

Turner, Ginger and Sarai Tiwari. *Abraham Lincoln: the Civil War President.* Gossamer Books LLC, 2004.

Wagner, Heather Lehr. *The Outbreak of the Civil War: A Nation Tears Apart.* Chelsea House, 2009.

Koestler-Grack, Rachel A. *Abraham Lincoln* (Leaders of the Civil War Era). Chelsea House Publishers, 2009.

Stanchak, John E. *Eyewitness Civil War.* (DK Eyewitness Books). Dorling Kindersley, 2011.

WEBSITES

www.civilwar.com
Comprehensive privately run, moderated site on the Civil War.

www.civil-war.net
Collection of images, written sources, and other material about the Civil War.

www.historyplace.com/civilwar
The History Place Civil War timeline.

www.pbs.org/civilwar
PBS site supporting the Ken Burns film The Civil War.

www.civilwar.si.edu
The Smithsonian Institution's Civil War collections, with essays, images, and other primary sources.

INDEX